How Saints are Canonised

by

Chri

GW00796142

*All booklets are published thanks to the
generous support of the members of the
Catholic Truth Society*

CATHOLIC TRUTH SOCIETY
PUBLISHERS TO THE HOLY SEE

Contents

Dedication

To my family, friends and the memory of Fr Joseph Eldridge, 1912-1993, priest of the Archdiocese of Westminster - a true example of the Christian Faith.

Introduction

In the Christian Calendar, November 1st is the feast of All Saints. This feast reminds Christians that through baptism they are called to be saints.

The pontificate of Pope John Paul II set many records, one being the numbers beatified and canonised during his 26 year reign. However, he was criticised for turning the Vatican into a saint producing factory. Such critics fail to grasp the nuances of the teachings of the Gospel and the Second Vatican Council on the nature of holiness.

All saints are held out as being worthy of veneration and imitation by Christians. Those who have been beatified are also examples of the Christian life. However, it is only human to be attracted to particular saints or blesseds. The great diversity of people that Pope John Paul II raised to the Altars (from simple people such as Mother Teresa, to other such as the Blessed Charles, Emperor of Austria) is truly surprising.

The saints and blesseds from all ages are remarkable examples of the Christian life which the Church holds out as models for living the Christian life. In following their example we can bring ourselves closer to our heavenly home.

This booklet is an introduction to the history and process of beatification and canonisation in the Catholic Church. Throughout history the process has changed as the Church has developed. We will look at beatification and canonisation in the early church, from locally approved cults of veneration to a more systematic approach in the Middle Ages; then to a more formal trial basis between 1643, up to 1983, when Pope John Paul II made major reforms which simplified the process.

The Sacred Congregation for the Causes of Saints published with Pope Benedict XVI's approval on 18th February 2008 a new instruction, *Sanctorum Mater,* which consolidates canonical practice over the last 20 years.

Beatification and canonisation in the early Church

Saints in the early Church were those who like St Stephen (*Ac* 6:11-14) were martyrs and were acclaimed as such by the local bishop. The early Church clearly understood the need to ensure that devotion was only paid to those who deserved honour after a process of investigation and official ecclesial approval. St Optatus of Mileve records an event from the fourth century, where the noble Lady Lucilla is rebuked by Caecilianus, Bishop of Carthage, for taking communion after having venerated the bones of a person who had not been acclaimed as a martyr.

Role of martyrs

The early Church understood that the Christian who followed Christ perfectly would go to heaven. Others would enter the purifying fires of purgatory "to be made perfect," from which they would not depart until they had "paid the last penny" (See *Mt* 5:26, 1 *Co* 3:13, 15). Since perfection was seen as conformity of one's life to the life of Christ, including the example of His death, a martyr was seen to have achieved the perfect imitation of

Christ. Therefore during the great age of persecution (from the first Pentecost to the Edict of Milan, 313) esteem for those Christians who had died a martyr's death led other Christians to extol their heroic witness to Christ, to guard and preserve their relics, and to celebrate the anniversary of their martyrdom as their entry into eternal life. The *Circular Letter of the Church of Smyrna* in the year 115 on the Martyrdom of St Polycarp illustrates this:

> "We have at last gathered his bones, which are dearer to us than priceless gems and purer than gold, and laid them to rest where it was befitting they should lie. And if it be possible for us to assemble again, may God grant us to celebrate the birthday of his martyrdom with gladness, thus to recall the memory of those who fought in the glorious combat, and to teach and strengthen by his example, those who shall come after us."

Paying respect to the venerable dead was also part of Jewish life. The Old Testament, shows that the prophet Hezekiah was honoured on his death (2 *Ch* 32:33). To this day altars in Catholic churches continue to be consecrated with relics of saints being placed into them.

Categories of martyrdom

Whilst there is only one fact of martyrdom, that is dying for the Catholic faith, there are five categories or circumstances in which martyrdom can occur:

1. *in odium fidei* - from hatred of the faith;
2. *in defensum castitatis* - in defense of chastity;
3. *ex aerumnis carceris* - from the hardships of incarceration;
4. *per testimonium caritatis fortis* - by witness of heroic charity;
5. *ex acertatibus et vexationibusque pro fidei quibus pertulit* - by reason of the force and violence which were endured for the faith.

In time Christianity became the official religion of the Roman Empire, and it became clear to the Church that people who were not martyrs, could also be fitting examples of the Christian life and canonised. These saints, such as St Martin of Tours (died 397) are called confessors. Churches were dedicated to the martyrs. However, Pope Symmachus (498-514) had dedicated two churches in Rome to St Sylvester and St Martin of Tours, both of whom were confessor saints. Canonisations were normally done quickly by public acclamation.

Beatification and canonisation: 313-1643

The Edict of Milan 313
and reforms of Pope Urban VIII 1643

These acclamations were generally made within a single diocese. But some martyrs and confessors had wider acclaim and spread to several dioceses or regions. Other figures such as Mary and the apostles had universal importance from the early days and were venerated as saints across the Christian world.

The call *santo subito*, "sainthood now", or canonisation by acclamation, was not restricted to the Church of the martyrs, nor indeed as an initiative from the faithful. When Clare of Assisi died in 1253, Pope Innocent IV was to celebrate her requiem mass and was on the verge of celebrating the mass of a virgin saint as opposed to the requiem mass, when he was advised by his entourage that this would constitute a *de facto* canonisation. Pope Innocent relented and Clare was eventually canonised after due process by Pope Alexander IV in 1255. So the calls of *santo subito* heard at the funeral of Pope John Paul II in April 2005 were not without precedent. However, the Church rightly does not depart radically from established due process.

Papal restrictions

While the early Church Councils show occasional interventions to correct abuses in naming saints and to establish criteria for their acclamation, the process continued to remain a local one. There are some few examples of popes declaring saints worthy of universal veneration.

Gradually, over time, the popes restricted the process of beatification and canonisation to the Holy See. Historians accept that Pope John XV was the first pope to canonise a saint in 993 during a Roman Synod, when he canonised St Ulric, Bishop of Augsburg (who was a non-martyr). One of the first canonical investigative processes initiated by the pope occurred under Pope Urban II, in the cause of Nicholas Peregrinus who died at Trani, Italy. The Bishop of Trani was required to conduct a local investigation into his reputation for sanctity and miracles, which then would be submitted to the Pope for judgment. St Nicholas, a young man, had been famous for travelling the countryside carrying a cross and singing *Kýrie eléison*: some contemporises considered him mad. However, he demonstrated miracles after death and was approved by Pope Urban II for canonisation in 1098. Thereafter Pope Callistus II (1119-1124) required all causes to include a critical biography of the Servant of God.

Process reserved to Pope

Full Roman supervision of the process was formalised by the reforms of Pope Alexander III, who forbade according ecclesial honour to anyone who had not received papal sanction. As often happens in the Church, abuses brought about major developments in Church practice. Pope Alexander III decreed in 1171 that no one could be declared a saint without the permission of the Supreme Pontiff. This was precipitated by one local church acclaiming as a martyr saint a man who had been killed while drunk. The pope's intervention focussed on the fact that being drunk, the man could not be said to have been a willing witness for Christ. It is from this intervention that papal approval or mandate for beatification becomes settled. This requirement was confirmed by Pope Innocent III in 1200 when he canonised St Cunegunde. The requirement was formally incorporated into Church law through the *Decretals* of Pope Gregory IX in 1234, which asserted that Rome alone had the right to beatify or canonise. The last beatification by a bishop appears to be that by the Archbishop of Malines, who beatified Boniface of Lausanne in 1603. Boniface was later canonised by Pope Clement in 1702.

Even before canonisation was reserved to the Holy See there is evidence that local churches deferred to Rome for papal approval for canonisations. Two English examples illustrate this. The first is King Offa of West Mercia who petitioned Pope Hadrian I to canonise St Alban.

The second is St Edward the Confessor. King Henry II petitioned Pope Alexander III to canonise him in 1161. Pope Alexander consented and said in his Bull of Canonisation:

> "Having seen the letters of Our predecessor, Pope Innocent of holy memory, and having received your evidence (he is referring to the English bishops), although so difficult and sacred a matter is rarely granted, save in a solemn synod, yet after counsel taken with Our brethren, according to the ardent desire of Our son the King (Henry II) and of all of you, we decree that the body of the Confessor be honoured and glorified with due rites upon earth, just as the Lord has already by His grace glorified him in heaven."

'Saint' or 'blessed'

During the Avignon Papacy (1305-1376), the popes further developed the beatification and canonisation process, which included advocates for and against the potential saint. They also distinguished between the titles of "blessed" and "saint." In 1512, Pope Julius II formalised the difference between beatification and canonisation as separate titles and stages of a judicial process. The essential difference is that a saint is venerated by the universal church and a blessed by the local church.

Pope Urban VIII in the Apostolic Constitution *Decreta servanda in beatificatione et canonizatione Sanctorum* 1642, asserted complete, full and final papal primacy in determining the procedure for beatifications and canonisations and who should be raised to the Altars. For nearly 200 years the "handbook" on the procedure was that written by Cardinal Prosper Lambertini (a noted canonist) who was elected pope in 1740 taking the name Pope Benedict XIV. This "handbook" was effectively incorporated into the Code of Canon Law, 1917.

Beatification and canonisation: 1640s-1930s

Between 1643 and 1930 the process of beatification and canonisation remained virtually unchanged (these dates are marked by the Constitution *Coelestis Hierusalem* of Pope Urban VIII on 5th July 1643, and the minor reforms of Pope Pius XII in 1930 in the *Motu Proprio Gia de qualctetempo*). The process was codified in the 1917 Code of Canon Law (canons 1999-2141).

The Code of Canon Law reaffirmed the sole jurisdiction of the Holy See to determine who should be beatified and canonised and the process to follow to bring a cause. The law also confirmed that the final decision was the Pope's alone (canon 1999).

The beatification and canonisation process was essentially divided into two. The first part was the ordinary process or non-cult; the second was the extraordinary process, or where there is a cult of veneration (canon 2000). In the ordinary process an investigation was conducted into the person's life to prove that:

　　a) they had lived a life of heroic virtue, or

　　b) they were martyred for the faith, and

　　c) miracles had been proved by them.

The extraordinary process arose where the person had already received a cult of veneration. This process only applied to those who had died one hundred years prior to the decree of Pope Urban VIII in 1643. Causes had to proceed on their own merits and could not be joined together unless they concerned martyrs who had either suffered on the same date or during the same period, such as the martyrs of the English reformation or the Spanish civil war (canon 2001).

The ordinary process is divided into the preparatory or preliminary process completed by the local bishop, and the apostolic process completed by the Holy See and confirmed by the Pope.

The ordinary process

The local bishop where the person died is asked by a group of the faithful to open a cause for beatification (canon 2003). Approval is given by the Sacred Congregation of Rites (the Congregation) to open the cause and a Postulator and Promoter of the Faith are appointed (the Postulator is considered at canon 2004 and the Promoter of the faith at canon 2010). Both office holders must be priests and must have a permanent residence in Rome. The Roman Postulator has authority to appoint vice-postulators in the diocese outside Rome to promote the cause. When the Congregation gives approval for an investigation the person is known as the 'Servant of God'. A cause should not be opened within the first 50 years of the person's death (canon 2101). However, many causes have been opened before then.

Preliminary invesigations

The task of the bishop is to oversee the preparatory phase which involves:

a) gathering the writings of the person;

b) collecting testimony as to the person's fame for holiness of life and living the Christian virtues, or that the person suffered martyrdom for the faith and that the person has worked *post mortem* miracles; and

c) establishing that no public veneration has been bestowed on the person.

The Postulator is charged with gathering the evidence and submitting it to the bishop for his approval (canon 2006).

Papers to Rome

Once the preliminary investigations have been completed, the bishop sends the sealed papers (called the *positio)* to the Congregation in Rome. When they are received in Rome, the Pope appoints a cardinal to be the Relator or *ponens* of the cause (canon 2009). The role of the Relator is to oversee the cause in Rome. He is to be present at all plenary and ordinary meetings of the Congregation of Rites concerning the cause, and he is to present all evidence positive and negative to these meetings. The Postulator of the cause is to confirm that all the stages have been completed properly. The Promoter of the Faith (a role termed the "Devil's Advocate" in the imagination of the public) is charged with raising reasonable objections to the cause.

Tribunal in diocese

The Congregation meets three times to review each of the three phases outlined above (canon 2102). The cause is voted on by the cardinals of the Congregation who submit a petition to the Pope to either approve or close the investigation. When the Pope approves the investigation he signs a decree instituting the Apostolic Process. This has the effect of returning the cause to the local bishop in order to establish a tribunal of five judges within his diocese so as to submit the cause to detailed investigation. These five judges will be supplemented by medical experts when considering miracles and will be attended by two sub-promoters of the faith (appointed by the Promoter of the faith in Rome). The process is effectively a trial. The trial must be completed within two years of the date that the letters of appointment are opened. If it does not, and more then a further two years elapse with little progress, the trial can only resume with the permission of the Congregation (canon 2095). The trial's remit is to establish proof of the following (canon 2104):

    a) the reputation of holiness of the person and that they lived a life of heroic virtue; or

    b) that they suffered martyrdom for the faith;

    c) that they have worked the required numbers of *post mortem* miracles.

It is the role of the Postulator to find this information. To support him he can ask the bishop to publish a notice in his diocese asking for evidence to support the information gathering (canon 2043). Where a person's reputation extends outside one diocese, the Postulator can request that the notice is published elsewhere (canon 2044). The code places a duty on all the faithful to provide evidence for or against the cause (canon 2023). Where this happens, the bishop in the other diocese is charged with proving the documents and sending them to the bishop in whose diocese the cause is initiated. It is also his role to present the Promoter of the Faith with a list of witnesses and issues on which he (the Promoter) is to question them.

During this process the judges visit the person's grave and lodgings and the person's remains are exhumed for identification (canon 2029).

The Promoter of the Faith is obligated to attend all sessions of the Congregation which discusses the cause. He is to ask questions which seek to elicit the truth of the matter. He submits his questions to the judges prior to questioning. The judges may also ask other questions and also call other witnesses (canon 2012). The Postulator may not be present during questioning.

Once the Apostolic process in the diocese is completed the bishop sends the cause to Rome under seal.

Cause goes to Rome

When the cause arrives in Rome, the Congregation first confirms that the diocesan Apostolic Process was properly conducted according to law. Next, the Cardinal Relator appoints examiners to examine the person's writings. These examiners must be priests who hold doctorates in theology (canon 2066). These examiners are appointed with the agreement of the Promoter of the Faith. Should the examiners find fault in the person's work the Pope may still allow the cause to be considered by the threefold congregational examination (canon 2071).

The Congregation subjects the cause to three separate examinations known as (canon 2101):

a) *Congregatio antepraeparatoria;*

b) *Congregatio praeparatoria;*

c) *Congregatio generalis.*

The *Congregatio antepraeparatoria* is a meeting of curial officials and the Cardinal *Ponens*. The *Congregatio praeparatoria* is a meeting of all the members of the Congregation of Rites and officials. The *Congregatio generalis* like the proceeding meeting is a full meeting of members and officials before the Pope and is presided over by the Pope.

Each element of the cause is subject to three separate examinations by the above congregations. This means that the evidence for heroic virtues or martyrdom is considered by the three congregations. If agreed by each congregation a decree is issued. If the *Congregatio antepraeparatoria* votes two thirds against the cause then the cause does not proceed to the following congregations without permission of the Pope (canon 2107). After this the proof of miracles is considered by the three congregations. The burden of proof is on the cause to prove to the congregations that it can vote with moral certainty that either the person lived the heroic virtues or that they suffered true martyrdom for the faith, and further that the miracles are without natural explanation. Moral certainty is a legal concept of proof which is similar to the requirement in English criminal law of proof beyond reasonable doubt.

The *Congregatio generalis* is a general meeting of the Congregation of Rites which meets before the Pope to discuss whether it is proper to beatify the person. The

Pope makes the final decisions (canon 2114). Once the Pope has accepted that the person has lived a life of heroic virtue or suffered martyrdom for the faith, he bestows the title Venerable on the Servant of God. The next step is to prove the required number of miracles in order to bestow the title Blessed on the person, which is done once the Pope accepts that the miracle is due to the intercession of the candidate (canon 2114).

Consideration of miracles for both stages

Both confessors and martyrs are required to show miracles, though with permission from the Pope such requirement for martyrs may be dispensed (canon 2116). Miracles must be *post mortem* and normally of a medical nature. Miracles performed during a person's life - such as healing, bi-location or knowing the secrets of a person's heart - whilst demonstrating a reputation for holiness, are insufficient to demonstrate the required miracles for the purpose of beatification. This is because the Church seeks miracles after death, going to show that the person is in heaven with the Father.

At least two miracles are needed for each stage of the process: two for beatification and two for canonisation. Three miracles may be required for each stage if the same witnesses give evidence in both the preliminary informative stage and the Apostolic stage. If the cause relies on historical events that can only be demonstrated by documents rather then eyewitness, the cause must demonstrate four miracles from historical documents which evidence the person's miraculous intervention (canon 2117).

The Cardinal Relator appoints at least two medical experts, specialists in the field of medicine, to consider whether the miracle is true and cannot be explained by natural healing. Where these experts disagree the Cardinal Relator appoints a further two experts to consider the issue. If no agreement to the claimed miracle is forthcoming, then the claim fails and another miracle must be found.

As with the claim of martyrdom or heroic virtues, the claimed miracle proceeds through the three Congregations to be considered by the Pope. The questions for each congregation are (canon 2119):

1. Was the person truly cured?
2. If so, can the cure be explained by natural causes?

The Congregations will also consider whether the cure is permanent and spontaneous. Only one miracle can be considered during the first and second congregation. More than one can be presented to the general congregation before the Pope who alone determines whether it is a miracle or not. If accepted, the Pope agrees to beatify the person. The beatification takes places in the person's home diocese.

Beatification by way of existing cult or the extraordinary process

To be considered for beatification by way of existing cult the person must have lived, died and had an existing cult of veneration between the pontificates of Pope Alexander III in 1171 and a hundred years prior to the decrees of Pope Urban VIII in 1634. The principal difference between the ordinary process and the extraordinary process is that evidence of existing cult must be proved whereas in the ordinary process existing cult must be suppressed (canon 2125). The process is as follows.

The bishop in whose diocese there is a tradition of veneration petitions the Congregation of Rites to open a cause (canon 2126). If approved the Congregation appoints a Postulator charged to:

1. gather and examine the person's writings;
2. demonstrate a consistent and historical veneration of the person in the region;
3. demonstrate the person's reputation for living the heroic virtues or suffering martyrdom and reputation for holiness and miracles.

The Postulator then submits the information to the bishop who forwards it to the Congregation. When received, the Pope appoints a Cardinal Relator to oversee the cause as he does in an ordinary cause. The difference is that a committee of experts is convened to consider whether the person has received consistent veneration (canon 2128). If the committee reports that the person has, the Congregation in ordinary session approves a petition to the Pope to open the Apostolic process.

The Apostolic process is instituted and the cause is subject to the same scrutiny as the ordinary process (canon 2133). The process seeks to demonstrate in addition that the person has received veneration since before the decrees of Pope Urban VIII (canon 2134). If the Pope confirms the proposition then the person is beatified (canon 2135).

Process before Paul VI

Prior to 1661, beatification was decided by the local bishop in conjunction with the group promoting the cause. The local bishop would set the date and the process of declaring the Blessed. Between 1661-1970s the process became more formal and solemn and was performed at St Peter's in Rome. The first "Roman beatification" in this solemn form appears to be that of Blessed Frances de Sales who was beatified on 8th January 1662 by Pope Alexander VII (and later canonised). Effectively the ceremony was in two parts on the same day. During the morning Mass, between the Penitential Rite and the Gloria, the Prefect of the

Congregation of Rites received the petition from the
Postulator of the cause and read out the concession of the
title of Blessed from the Pope from the Bull of
Beatification (promulgated on 28th December 1661).
Next, the bishop of the Blessed's diocese read out the
biography of the new Blessed and after that the Prefect
confirmed the title under papal mandate that Frances was
now a Blessed of the Church. The Mass was celebrated
by the Bishop of Soissons, the diocese which had
promoted the cause of Frances. In the afternoon of the
same day, Pope Alexander entered St Peter's Basilica to
venerate the new Blessed and to receive the indulgence
for so doing.

This was the process until Pope Paul VI decided to
preside at the beatification Mass, which meant that the
afternoon rite was abolished. Pope Paul VI presided at
the beatification of Maximillian Kolbe on 17th October
1971 (later canonised on 10th October 1982 by Pope
John Paul II). The rite was similar to that introduced by
Pope Alexander, however, and the petition or *peroratio*
asking for beatification was read out by the Prefect of the
Congregation for the Causes of Saints and then the local
bishop read out the biography of the new blessed. The
pope then approved the beatification and Mass
proceeded with the Gloria.

Canonisation

The historical process of canonisation was as follows. The Postulator of the cause petitions the Congregation for approval to introduce the canonisation cause. To start with the Congregation establishes that the person has been beatified. The Congregation will consider the issue in ordinary meeting and submit to the Pope that the person has been beatified (canon 2136).

In the case of a formally beatified person (or a person beatified by the ordinary process) two miracles occurring after the date of beatification must be proved (canon 2136). In the case of a person beatified by the extraordinary process, three miracles are required.

If the Pope agrees to the resumption of the cause, he approves a decree from the Congregation stating this. The cause follows the same process as that in the beatification process. The claimed miracles in turn go through the three tribunals at the Congregation and if passed, then the Pope considers the votes of the Cardinals and determines whether to approve the canonisation (canon 2140).

If approved the Pope presides at the canonisation ceremony in Rome (canon 2141). Whilst the Pope alone determined who was to be raised to the Altars, saints were not always canonised in Rome. Prior to the pontificate of Benedict XIII (who canonised St Stanislas Kostkla in Rome in 1726 and then ruled that all canonisations

should be held in Rome) canonisations occurred
elsewhere. For example, St Edmund of Canterbury was
canonised by Pope Innocent IV in 1247 at Lyons. St
Thomas of Hereford and St Thomas Aquinas were
canonised at Avignon by Pope John XXII in 1320 and
1323 respectively.

Whilst Pope John Paul II made substantive changes to
the process in 1983, important changes were also made
by Pope Pius XI and Pope Paul VI. These changes
affected the duplicate recognition process whereby the
candidate's life and virtues were examined through the
ordinary process and then the Apostolic process. Pope
Pius XI abolished the Apostolic process for historical
cases; i.e. those beyond living memory (*Normae
servandae in construendis processibus historici super
causis historicis* 1939). Pope Paul VI abolished the
Apostolic process in respect to all cases (*Sanctitar
clarior,* 1969), which meant that the local bishop became
responsible for conducting a combined ordinary/
Apostolic or single process after approval for the
introduction of the cause was given by the Holy See.

Modern times: 1900-1983

The twentieth century was a momentous century for the world and the church. The coming together of the world's bishops at the Second Vatican Council (1962-965) was very significant for the Catholic Church.

A key concern of the bishops at the Council was the reform of the Roman Calendar and the liturgy which by this time had become quite complicated. The intention of the bishops was to give priority to Sundays, the feasts days of Jesus Christ and important saints:

"Lest the feasts of the saints should take precedence over the feasts which commemorate the very mysteries of salvation, many of them should be left to be celebrated by a particular Church or nation or family of religious; only those should be extended to the universal Church which commemorates saints who are truly of universal importance." (Constitution on the Divine Liturgy *Sacrosanctum Concilium* 111)

Changes to Church calendar

These concerns were taken up by Pope Paul VI in the *Motu Proprio Mysterii Paschalis* which implemented the

Council's changes to the Roman Calendar in 1969. This streamlining was welcome since the Calendar at the time had complex criteria for assessing the priority of feast days which meant that a saint's day could often take priority over a Sunday. Prior to the reforms, feast days were prioritised as follows: simple, semi-double and double. The rank of double was further divided as double of the first class, double of the second class, greater double and major double and double. The reforms of the Council simplified this to memorial, feast and solemnity.

As a result, public veneration of many saints was removed from the Catholic Calendar of Saints: such as St Christopher and St Philomena (through St Philomena was removed prior to the Council in 1961 and St Christopher after the Council in 1969). Some commentators say that they were withdrawn from the universal calendar because they were not 'formally canonised' by the Church. However, St Christopher is considered to have been martyred under the Emperor Decius in the third century; St Philomena was martyred in the fourth century. Whilst the Church had a process in place at the time of their deaths, they would have been acclaimed by their local community and bishop as martyrs. So the phrase 'formally canonised' has less meaning when compared to the modern process.

Effect of canonisation

Formality of the process apart, are canonisations protected by the doctrine of infallibility? The doctrine is that when the Pope by a definitive act invokes the charism of infallibility in teaching on an issue of faith or morals that the Holy Spirit protects that statement from error and it then becomes part of Catholic teaching. Whilst the doctrine was only defined at the First Vatican Council (in the document *Pastor Aeternus)*, it nonetheless has scriptural basis in the New Testament when Christ names Peter as the Rock and head of the Church to whom he commits the keys of the Kingdom and the ability to bind or loosen in heaven and earth (*Mt* 16:18-19).

The doctrine has its canonical effect in the Code of Canon Law 1983, canon 749 which says that the Pope can exercise infallibility by virtue of his office and bishops if they are in communion with him. The Code is clear that to be infallible the act must be definitive i.e. clear and meant to be. The canon draws inspiration from Second Vatican Council (Dogmatic Constitution on the Church, *Lumen Gentium* Para 25).

The Congregation for the Doctrine of the Faith stated that canonisations were held to be definitive as they were "...truths connected to revelation by historical necessity and which are to be held definitively, but are not able to be declared as divinely revealed." (Doctrinal Commentary on the Concluding Formula of the *Profession Fidei 1998*).

Reforms of Pope John Paul II

In 1983, Pope John Paul II reformed the laws governing causes of beatification and canonisation (*Divinus Perfectionis Magister*). The laws effectively simplified the process mainly by reducing the number of miracles for each stage of the process from two to one. A martyr only needs to demonstrate a miracle for canonisation. These laws focus on a more inquisitorial approach, ensuring that process is followed to ensure that evidence is properly collected and considered. The current law retains the key officials of the Promoter of the Faith who is to study the cause in such a way that, before the *positio* is submitted for discussion in their special meeting, controversial theological questions, if there be any, may be examined thoroughly. In addition, the Promoter of the Faith is explicitly charged with resolving any controversial issue that may arise during the process. The cause cannot proceed until such time as the Promoter has resolved any issues of controversy. Along with the Promoter of Justice (who is to be appointed in the diocese for penal cases, and for contentious cases in which the public good may be at stake. The Promoter is bound by his office to safeguard the public good, which means that he is charged with ensuring suitable causes proceed). The role of these officials is to provide a critical eye. The final key official is the Relator who is responsible for presenting the cause to the Cardinal members of the Congregation for the Causes of Saints for their vote.

New instructions 2008

In February 2008, Pope Benedict XVI, through the Congregation for the Causes of Saints, issued new instructions. The Instruction, *Sanctorum Mater,* does not repudiate the laws of John Paul II, rather they reinvigorate them. The Instruction will be considered further when we look at the reforms of Pope Benedict XVI.

The current law therefore requires rigorous examination of the person's life, based on research and documentation to verify the reputation for holiness of the candidate rather then a judicial process. The requirement to robustly research the life of the candidate for beatification has been underlined by the Second Vatican Council which said "careful investigation - theological, historical and pastoral" should always be made where matters of public worship such as the veneration of the saints are involved: "the accounts of martyrdom or the life of the saints are to accord with the facts of history." (*Sacrosanctum Concilium* 23).

These reforms have been criticised by some who have interpreted the reduction in the number of required miracles as a reduction of the special nature of holiness and sanctity. However, the Council underlined the universal call to holiness that each Christian is called to live (Dogmatic Constitution on the Church, *Lumen Gentium*, Chapter V Universal Call to Holiness in the Church, para 39). It is clear from the teaching of Jesus in the Gospel that holiness and sanctity should be the norm of the Christian life. Indeed St Paul often addressed his letters to the saints/members of various church communities he founded (*Ph* 1:1).

Variety of saints

Pope John Paul II has highlighted the diversity of heaven. He canonised men, women and children from almost every country, culture and class; not just priests and nuns, but peasants, slaves and emperors. He invites us all to remember that we are all called to be saints. Pope John Paul II used beatifications and canonisations on his pastoral visits around the world to highlight the universality of holiness: that the biblical message is for all regardless of race, gender or station in life (*Ga* 3:27-29). The itinerant, the married couple or the lay person can be as worthy an example of holiness as the more traditional model of the religious or clergy. Pope John Paul II raised up examples of

holiness in every corner of the world so that people may
have true examples of Christian holiness in their own
cultures. For instance, he beatified the first gypsy, Ceferino
Jimenez Malla, also known as El Pele; the first married
couple, Luigi Quattrochi and Maria Corsini; he beatified
and canonised many examples of laity such as St Genna
Beretta Molla, a young wife, mother and professional
women who died in childbirth.

Timescales

Prior to the Council and the reforms of Pope John Paul II,
canonical custom and practice had established the
tradition that 50 years should elapse between a person's
death and the introduction of their cause for beatification.
Pope John Paul II reduced this period to five years. This
reduction in time ensures that we have contemporary
examples of holiness. Objections that this reduces the
concept of holiness over time, may be misplaced when
one considers how often Rome has reformed the process.
For instance Pope Pius XI established within the Sacred
Congregation of Rites a historical section to study
historical cases (*Motu Proprio, Gia de qualcte tempo,*
1930). Pope Pius XI in respect to historical cases
abolished the "Roman recognition" stage (*Normae
servandae in constrendid processibus ordinaries super
causis historics* 1939). Pope Paul VI extended the 1939

decree to all causes so that both historical and recent causes would have a single recognition process conducted by the local bishop (*Sanctita Clarior* 1969).

The reforms of Pope Alexander III in the 1170s were geared to facilitate a process of swift investigation and canonisation: for instance St Thomas Becket, Archbishop of Canterbury, who was murdered in 1170 was canonised in 1173. St Francis died in October 1226 and was canonised in July 1228. Quicker still was the canonisation of St Anthony of Padua who was canonised by Pope Gregory IX on 30th May 1232 some 352 days after his death.

Even under the previous law there are numerous examples of causes being introduced prior to the 50 years 'cooling off' period. The cause for St Thérèse of Lisieux (1873-1897) was opened by Pope Pius X who dispensed with the 50 year waiting period; she was beatified in 1923 and canonised in 1925. Whereas St Josemaría Escrivá who died in 1975 was beatified in 1992 and canonised in 2002. Other examples where the cause was opened or completed within 50 years included:

- St Gabriel Possenti (1883-1862): canonised in 1920, his cause was introduced in 1881.
- St Gemma Galgaria (1878-1903): canonised in 1940, her cause was introduced in 1917.
- St Maria Goretti (1890-1902): canonised in 1950, within 48 years of her death.

- Pope Pius X (1835-1914): canonised in 1954, his cause was introduced in 1923.

However, not all causes have been so quick. Two very slow ones were that of St Margaret Cortona who died in 1297 and was canonised by Pope Benedict XIII in 1728 some 431 years after her death. However, St Joan of Arc who died in 1431, was canonised by Pope Benedict XV in 1920 some 489 years after her death.

The swiftness or delay in canonisation is no reflection on the ultimate holiness of the person; rather it is, among other things, indicative of the ability of the cause to be promoted and gain momentum.

The Modern process: post 1983

No cause can be opened within the first five years of a person's death. The requirement to wait five years before opening a cause for beatification is a prudent step for three reasons:

a) It continues to allow a period of time to allow emotions to settle.

b) It enables the cause to receive evidence from the person's peers and contempories, rather than relaying of historical evidence.

c) It enables the Church to raise up contemporary examples of holiness for the modern world (and is more in tune with the previous historical norm of prompt canonisations).

Where more than thirty years have elapsed, no cause may be opened without the bishop being assured of just reasons for the delay.

No cause can be introduced unless there is a clear fame or reputation for holiness or martyrdom of the person concerned; but this reputation must not be public veneration. This has recently been reiterated by the 2008 Instruction of Pope Benedict XVI.

The process for considering causes for beatification and canonisation is as follows:

Stage 1: The Diocesan Stage

The bishop of the diocese where the candidate for beatification died opens a cause. Normally the introduction of the cause represents a ground swell of opinion on the merits of the deceased by a group of the faithful. Prior to opening the cause, the bishop should consult with the bishops of the region to see if such a cause should be introduced. Once the bishop agrees to open the cause a petition is presented to the Pope who, through the Congregation for the Causes of Saints signifies his agreement to opening the cause by issuing a *Nihil Obstat* signalling that the cause is formally opened. The person is given the title 'Servant of God' and so can be known as, for instance, the 'Servant of God Pope John Paul II'. There is nothing to stop the Promoter of the cause from conducting initial investigations prior to the granting of the *Nihil Obstat*; however, the formal process cannot start within five years of the person's death. Nevertheless, the Pope can reduce or completely dispense with this waiting period. In recent years the waiting period has been waived in the following causes:

- Mother Theresa of Calcutta (1910-1997): beatified in 2003 by Pope John Paul II.

- Sister Lucia (of Fatima) (1907-2005): opened in 2008 by Pope Benedict XVI.
- Pope John Paul II (1920-2005): opened in May 2005 by Pope Benedict XVI.

Once the cause is opened a Postulator is appointed by the bishop. The Postulator is the person who oversees the process of collecting evidence (including assessing the person's published works, such as books or sermons and private papers such as letters and diaries), and interviewing witness. The role of the Postulator is to ensure that the external life of the candidate as seen by people, was a true reflection of the internal virtue and life of the person. The law provides that the Postulator must have appropriate qualifications, such as being expert in theology, historical method and canon law. The Postulator may be male or female, cleric, religious or lay provided they have these required qualifications (Congregation for the Causes of Saints *New Laws for the Causes of Saints* 1983, para 3(a)).

The Instruction *Sanctorum Mater* requires that where possible, witness are eyewitnesses, and that questions are posed to elicit the truth and not to cover over anything that is unsupportive of the cause. It also provides that where a candidate is a member of a religious order, then most of the witness must be from outside of the order. The Instruction reiterates that confessors and spiritual directors should not give evidence.

As part of the diocesan process the body is exhumed in order to formally identify the remains. History recounts numerous blessed and saints whose mortal physical remains have remained incorrupt, that is that their bodies have not decayed. Joan Carroll Cruz in her book *The Incorruptibles* provides a biography of several well known cases such as St Bernadette of Lourdes and St John Vianney.

In modern times during the beatification process of the seers of Fatima, on exhumation in 1935 and 1951 the body of Jacinta Marto was found to be incorrupt. Incorruption is a mark of holiness but is not conclusive. Jacinta's brother Francisco was not found to be incorrupt though he like his sister was beatified by Pope John Paul II on 13th May 2000.

Purpose of the diocesan stage

The purpose of the diocesan stage is to prove the following:

a) that the person lived a life of heroic Christian virtue. The heroic virtues are a) the theological virtues of faith, hope and charity and b) the Christian virtues of prudence, justice, temperance and fortitude; and

b) in the case of a martyr, that they met their death as a true martyr (that is that the aggressor acted from motives of *odium fidei* [hatred for the faith] or *odium Ecclesiae* [hatred of the Church or its teachings]); or

c) in the case of a non-martyr, a miracle granted through the intercession of the person.

Since the reforms of Pope Paul VI in 1969, there is only one stage for the recognition of the virtues in the person's life, namely the diocesan stage. During this stage the bishop appoints an official termed the Promoter of Justice, who is appointed to prepare questions for the witnesses on the life the candidate and see to it that the investigation is carried out with due rigour and in accord with Canon Law (*New Laws for the Causes of Saints*, para 6(b)).

Once the Postulator has compiled a report known as a *positio* on the person's life, and the bishop consents, the diocesan process is completed and the cause is passed to Rome.

Proof of miracles

For a non-martyr, the Postulator will also need to prove a miracle that the person has worked after death, demonstrating their intercession before God to support the cause of beatification. If this is outside the diocese of death then the local bishop of that diocese will need to convene a commission to investigate the miracle.

The Instruction *Sanctorum Mater* requires two medical experts to examine the person healed using clinical and technical means to demonstrate the nature of the healing. This augments the requirements of the law that the bishop of the diocese in which the miracle occurred is responsible for establishing a tribunal of two sub-committees (one scientific and the other theological) to consider the miracle. The task of the tribunal is to establish:

a) whether a miracle has occurred; and

b) if a miracle has occurred, that it is due to the intercession of the candidate, thereby establishing that the person is in heaven.

The scientific sub-committee assesses the claimed miracle by accepted scientific criteria. (The Church normally considers miracles which are medical in nature). The sub-committee will examine what the condition was and what treatment has been given. It considers whether the cure has been or could have been affected by natural means, unknown natural causes or the result of therapeutic interventions. The sub-committee would also consider how the healing occurred and its permanency. Once the sub-committee has considered all the evidence, it then declares (as appropriate) that the cure has no natural explanation and is therefore a "miracle".

Once the scientific sub-committee has concluded that the cure has no natural causes the theological sub-committee considers how the cure occurred, in order to exclude the possibility of natural and unforeseen cures/remissions. Both sub-committees normally prefer cases where the patient's illness is beyond all medical help and that the cure occurs more or less instantly. For instance, Jack Traynor was cured at Lourdes in 1923. Seriously injured in 1916 during World War I, he suffered from epilepsy, the muscles in his right arm had atrophied and he had an inch wide metal plate in his skull covering the brain. The Lourdes Medical Bureau considered his healing in 1929 and found that on the day of his healing in 1923 the hole in his head was healed and his right arm was returned to full functioning. In addition he had not suffered an epileptic fit since 1923.

The theological sub-committee rules whether it is a strict miracle. Next, it considers how it came about. To do this the sub-committee will determine who the family and friends have prayed to. If they have solely been praying to the candidate then it can be concluded that the person has interceded with God on behalf of the patient. Where people have been praying to others such as the Blessed Mother or another saint then the issue becomes clouded and uncertain and will not proceed.

If both sub-committees accept that a miracle has occurred and the bishop consents, the bishop forwards the report to Rome for its consideration.

The Instruction *Sanctorum Mater* deals mainly with the diocesan phase and leaves the Roman stage very much as Pope John Paul II had established in *Divinius perfectionis magister* which we will look at now.

Stage 2: the Roman Stage

The Congregation for the Causes of Saints receives the *positio* on the life of the person and also the report from the diocese in respect to the miracle. The Congregation subjects each cause to a rigorous examination. Part of this examination is by a panel of nine theologians. The theologians are charged with ensuring that there is nothing contrary to faith and morals in the person's life and works. When the deliberations are concluded they vote. In order to proceed the cause must receive a majority vote from the theologians. If they vote in favour then the cause is considered by the Cardinals and Bishops (drawn from all over the world) who are members of the Congregation for the Causes of Saints. The members meet twice a month to consider and vote on causes. During this time a second Postulator will be appointed who must reside in Rome. Along with the appointment of a new Postulator residing in Rome, the Congregation will also appoint an official called the Promoter of the Faith. Like the Postulator he will be an expert in the workings of the Congregation, theology, canon law and historical method. The role of the Promoter of the Faith is to verify controversial issues and to give an opinion on them to the Congregation membership. Essentially the Promoter of the Faith fulfils a similar role in safeguarding the system from disrepute by ensuring that causes are free from error and that any problems are resolved and explained. He has the right to attend all the sessions and to receive reports where he cannot attend.

The Congregation will also examine whether the person lived a life of heroic virtue. For a non-martyr the Congregation will also review the evidence supporting the miracle and this is done by a panel of medical experts. The panel of nine theologians also considers whether the person has lived a life of heroic virtue In cases of martyrdom, the miracle required for beatification is waived, as martyrdom is traditionally understood as a miracle of grace in itself. In this case, the vote of the Congregation would establish the death of the Servant of God as true martyrdom, resulting in a Decree of Martyrdom by the Holy Father.

Once the cause has passed through the medical scrutiny and the theologians have voted, then the cause is passed to the Membership of the Congregations to consider. If the cause is passed then the Prefect of the Congregation presents the findings to the Pope who alone makes the decision to approve the beatification of the person.

Venerable: life of heroic virtue

The title of Venerable is conferred by the Pope once he has ruled positively that the person has lived a life of heroic virtue or has died a martyr's death. Such persons are called Venerable: for instance the 'Venerable Cardinal John Henry Newman' (1801-1890) or the 'Venerable Margaret Sinclair' (1900-1925).

With the Pope's approval that the person has lived a life of heroic virtue and, where applicable, approval that there has been a miracle, the Congregation issues a decree declaring the person 'Blessed' and a date is set for their beatification. With the beatification rite, the Venerable Servant of God is declared Blessed: for instance, 'Blessed Teresa of Calcutta'. Once beatified the person may receive liturgical veneration:

1. A Mass in their honour.
2. An office in the Divine Office.
3. Images in churches or the dedication of a church in their name.

The veneration of a Blessed is normally restricted to a particular geographical location or religious community such as the Beatified martyrs of England and Wales or Blessed Kateri Tekakwitha in the Americas, or Blessed

Titus Brandsma within the Carmelite order. With the Indult (permission) of the Sacred Congregation for the Discipline of Sacraments and Divine Worship, other dioceses and institutes may be granted the right to venerate the beatified person. Without such permission public veneration is unlawful outside the specific geographical territory or institution. This is because whilst the Pope approves a person for beatification, the Rite of beatification does not involve the Pope in an exercise of papal infallibility. Therefore it is not appropriate that the entire Church give public liturgical veneration to the person. The Christian faithful are however, permitted to invoke the person in private devotion (and of course report any favours to the Blessed's Postulator).

Veneration

The veneration of the saints and blesseds in the Catholic Church should not be confused with the worship that God alone is entitled to. The Church teaches that God is the Lord and God of the living, and therefore the Church teaches that after the death of the body, comes the after life. The saints and blesseds are held out as being guides for the inspiration and imitation of all. The Church regards the saints and blesseds as deserving of respect, devotion and imitation (*dulia*). Whilst the Church pays special respect and devotion to the Blessed Virgin Mary and accords her high honour as the mother of Christ (*hyperdulia*), only God as the Father and creator of the universe is worshipped. Beatification or canonisation is not an honour bestowed by the Church in the sense of earthly honours, such as honours due to a specific office, or the tradition in Ancient Rome or Egypt of deification of the emperor or pharaoh. The Church merely declares what God has already decreed that these men, women and children are worthy of veneration and imitation.

We see in the Bible the acceptance of paying respect or veneration to others. The best example is that of honouring mother and father, found in the Ten Commandments (*Ex* 20:2-17). Jesus also commends that we respect mother and father (*Mt* 15:4).

In Genesis, Lot venerates an Angel by bowing to the ground (*Gn* 19:1). The brothers of Joseph also bow to him, as does Saul to Samuel (see *Gn* 42:6, 1 *S* 28:14 respectively).

Paul commands us to venerate the saints and receive honour through this veneration (1 *Co* 11:1). Respect was not only paid by humans to human or humans to angels. In the case of Mary the mother of Jesus, we see that the Archangel Gabriel at the Annunciation honoured Mary by saying "Hail full of grace…" (*Lk* 1:28).

Benedict XVI process

Pope Benedict XVI has made several adjustments to the process of beatification and canonisation. Quite soon after his election he departed from the practice of Pope John Paul II, by returning to a more traditional model where the rite/ceremony of beatification is carried out by the Prefect of the Congregation for the Causes of Saints, or by the designated bishop in the home diocese of the candidate. The beatifications by Cardinal Jozef Clemp of Ignatius Klopotowski the founder of the Congregation of the Sisters of the Blessed Virgin Mary of Loretto in Warsaw on 19th June 2005; Cardinal Jose Saraiva Martins, Prefect of the Congregation of the Causes of Saints, beatifying Cardinal Clemens August Graf Von Galen in Germany on 9th October 2005 would be examples of this return to the traditional approach.

Pope Benedict XVI has returned to the early tradition of the Church whereby beatification takes place in the locality of the person, under papal mandate and approval. He has also honoured the teaching of his predecessor Pope John Paul II who said "in the light of the doctrine of the Second Vatican Council on collegiality, we also think the Bishops themselves should be more closely associated with the Holy See in dealing with the Causes of Saints." (*Divinius Perfectionis Magister* introductory comments).

In the Rite of Beatification under Pope Benedict XVI, the Pope appoints a delegate to represent him at the beatification taking place in the home diocese of the person to beatified. Where several persons are to be beatified, then the ceremony is held in a suitable part of the region. The delegate is normally the Prefect of the Congregation for the Causes of Saints. The Rite takes place during the Mass, between the Penitential Rite and the Gloria. The local bishop presents the *perationo*, the Prefect reads the papal mandate to raise the new blessed to the Altar and then the local bishop reads the biography of the new blessed. The Mass then continues as normal from the Gloria. Where more than one new blessed is announced, these steps are repeated for each candidate.

These changes to the Rite of Beatification restore the traditional distinction between beatification and canonisation. Whereas beatification is an act of the local church whereby the Blessed is venerated in the local church, canonisation is an act of the Pope and entitles a person declared a saint to universal veneration. These changes also promote the role of the local church in honouring their local people. This important aspect of beatification was at risk of being blurred when both Pope Paul VI and Pope John Paul II presided at beatifications. Once beatified, the next stage for the candidate is to commence the cause of canonisation, which is essentially a search for a second miracle.

Stage 3: Diocesan consideration of the second miracle

As in the case of the miracle required for beatification, where a second miracle is proposed, the bishop in whose diocese the claim is made, appoints a tribunal of two sub-committees (as we have seen above) to test whether the miracle is a true miracle and whether it is due to the intercession of the Blessed. After the tribunal has approved the miracle and the bishop consents, the bishop forwards a report to Rome.

Stage 4: Roman Stage

After the diocesan process has concluded, the proposed miracle is studied both by a scientific and by a theological Commission of the Congregation for the Causes of Saints. The vote of this Commission is forwarded to the members of the Congregation whose affirmative vote is then communicated to the Pope. The consent of the Pope to the decision of the Congregation results in a Decree confirming that the miracle has occurred, and thus the road to canonisation is opened.

Stage 5: Canonisation

In the Rite of Canonisation the Pope exercises infallibility and elevates the Blessed to Sainthood, thus allowing universal veneration of the new Saint by the Church. By canonisation the Pope does not *make* the person a *saint*. Such people were already formed into saints by God; canonisation merely reveals that the person in question is a saint with God in heaven. As such they are worthy of veneration and imitation by the faithful. Once a saint is canonised they are entitled to the following:

1. They will be given a Feast Day in the Roman Calendar.
2. They may have Churches throughout the World dedicated to them.
3. Their Relics may be venerated publicly.
4. Other public acts of veneration such as a novena.

While most new saints have a feast day in the Roman Calendar, the feast day is not universally observed. However, if the saint has universal appeal they may be added to the general Roman Calendar as a Memorial or Optional Memorial. If their appeal is limited to a particular region, nation, or religious institute, the saint may be added to the particular calendars of those nations or institutes. However, it is possible for clergy and faithful outside those areas who have a devotion to the saint, to mark their feast day with a votive Mass or Office without the need for an *Indult* (special permission).

The current law, as before allows for beatification or canonisation by way of existing cult. So, like many of his predecessors, Pope John Paul II had formally approved the existing cult of certain people, (eg. Blessed Dun Scotus (1266-1308) in 1993). Approval of cult continues to be a process whereby the Pope approves the cult of veneration of a person who has died at least one hundred years prior to the coming into force of the decree of Pope Urban VIII in 1643. Where the Pope approves the beatification or canonisation of a person this is known as an *equipollent* or equivalent beatification or canonisation. It is regarded as being equivalent to one carried out after Pope Urban's 1643 reforms, as it involves a due process of investigation carried out by the local bishop and the Congregation in order demonstrate that the person had received a cult of veneration since "time immemorial". After the Congregation confirms this, the Pope issues a decree which confirms existing cult of veneration.

Canonisation is an act of the Pope, and for that reason Pope Bendict XVI continues to preside over the Rite. The Rite (as for beatification) is conducted between the Pentitential Rite and the Gloria of the Canonisation Mass.

The Rite is as follows. The Prefect of the Congregation for the Causes of Saints, accompanied by the Consistorial Advocate and the Postulators, addresses the Holy Father with these words: "Our Holy Mother Church asks Your Holiness to count the Blessed(s) [name], as Saint(s) and thus [they] will be known and venerated by all Christians." The Prefect then reads the life of the Blessed in brief.

The Rite concludes when the Pope declares:

"For the glory of the Holy Trinity, the exaltation of the Catholic faith, the spreading of the Christian faith, and with the authority of Our Lord Jesus Christ, the Apostles Saints Peter and Paul, and our own, after a long discernment where God's help was invoked, and our venerable brother archbishops' advice was taken into consideration, we declare the Blessed(s) [name] as Saint(s), and we include [them] in the list of saints and we ascertain their veneration as saints within the Church. In the Name of the Father, and of the Son, and of the Holy Spirit. Amen."

The Mass proceeds as usual, with the singing of the Gloria.

Differences between historical and modern process

Prior to the reforms of Pope John Paul II there were minor amendments by Popes Pius XI and Paul VI which effectively combined the informative stage and Apostolic stages, mentioned earlier, into one 'recognition' stage.

The most obvious difference between the new and the former process is the "cooling off" period, before a cause could be introduced. The reduction from 50 to five years means that causes can be introduced sooner so as to present more contemporary examples of the Christian life to be imitated by the faithful. As we have seen, both time-limits could be dispensed with to allow causes to be introduced earlier: for instance, formerly, St Therese of Lisieux; recently, Mother Teresa.

Another difference concerns requirements for miracles. Formerly at least two miracles for each stage, and currently only one for each stage were required. Pope Pius XII established the Medical Commission in the 1940s which ensured that miracles were subjected to vigorous examination.

The process maintains the same participants, but with some key changes. Women are now allowed to promote a cause. In the 1917 Code of Canon Law women had to act through a proxy. The cause is still passed into the hands of a Relator whose role is to present the cause to the Congregation and promote it. The current law no longer requires the Relator to be a cardinal. The Postulator now may also be a woman.

The roles of the Promoter of the faith and of other officials, such as notaries and attorneys who all act to ensure a cause is properly considered, remain.

Reforms of Pope Benedict XVI

In February 2008 the Congregation for the Causes of Saints issued an Instruction entitled *Sanctorum Mater*. This instruction, approved by Pope Benedict XVI in April 2006 and published in the Church's official record known as *Acta Apostolicae Sedis* in June 2007, builds on Pope Benedict XVI's reform of the Rite of Beatification and sets down clear directions on how the local church should conduct enquiries for the Causes of Saints.

The Instruction has been portrayed by some as an effort to slow down the rate of canonisations, as for example took place under Pope John Paul II who beatified 1,337 and canonised 482 persons over his lengthy pontificate. Comparing the first three years of the pontificates of Pope John Paul II and Pope Benedict XVI, we see that in the period 18th October 1978 to 18th October 1981 Pope John Paul II beatified 33 people and canonised two saints. In the three year period 19th April 2005 to the 19th April 2008 Pope Benedict has beatified 563 people and canonised 14 saints. While the Congregation has been working to the more streamlined process introduced by Pope John Paul II, each pope is the final arbiter and may dispense with the canonical norms where he deems it opportune. The view that the Instruction may be a repudiation of Pope John Paul's reforms, and a slowing down process, indicates a more secular view of holiness, sanctity, and of the work of the Holy Spirit in bearing fruits. It may well arise from a misplaced distrust of the Church to properly scrutinise causes for beatification and canonisation.

Purpose of new instructions

The Prefect of the Congregation for the Causes of Saints, at the launch of the Instruction, confirmed that its purpose was to reinvigorate the existing law. The Instruction is aimed at the local church. It stresses the need for clarity and certainty in opening causes to ensure that causes are only opened for those who have truly lived a life of heroic virtue or genuine martyrdom. Like *Divinius perfectionis magister,* the Instruction focusses on the central role of the bishop in guiding the introduction of causes as well as the need to discourage the notion that every cause introduced will by necessity reach either the beatification or canonisation. The Instruction was issued to enable bishops to properly manage beatification causes. Many causes arrived at the Congregation not having been scrutinised properly. Many dioceses lack sufficient experts to properly investigate causes, thus resulting in the Congregation having to seek clarifications. The Instruction therefore is really a "practice" manual to ensure that causes are properly conducted and to reduce the number of clarifications the Congregation seeks. It comprises six sections dealing with the diocesan phase of opening a cause for beatification. The sections consider the following:

- Section One: no cause is to be opened without there being an apparent reputation for holiness in the person. There should also be no public veneration of the person.

- Section Two: considers the role of the bishop from the opening of the initial investigation to receiving the *Nihil Obstat* of the Congregation to formally open the cause.

- Section Three: instructs the local bishop on how he is to conduct enquiries in beatification and canonisation causes.

- Section Four: deals with the gathering of documentary evidence, such as letters and books.

- Section Five: deals with the questioning of witnesses. Questions to witness should be clear and concise and asked in a manner which elicits factual answers. Witnesses are to demonstrate how they can be sure of the evidence that they give. Where witnesses give evidence which is negative, this evidence must be fully assessed and responded to.

- Section Six: considers the closing of the diocesan
  phase and the forwarding of the cause to Rome.

Consolidation

The Instruction is not a repudiation of *Divinius perfectionis
magister;* rather it consolidates the practice and experience
of those involved in this important process of the Church
since 1983. It incorporates the recent initiatives of Pope
Benedict XVI to promote the role of the local church by
returning to the historical practice of beatification. The
Instruction is essentially a reminder that promoting
candidates for beatification and canonisation is a
responsible task which needs to be conducted in a rigorous
manner. The Instruction does this by reinvigorating the
principles of *Divinius perfectionis magister* which has been
in operation since 1983. It highlights the need to conduct a
thorough examination and also to guard against the
assumption that any cause introduced will ultimately result
in a beatification and canonisation.

At the same time as publishing the Instruction, the
Congregation also published the latest edition of the
Index ac Status Causarum. This index lists the
outstanding causes pending at the Congregation: there are
in the region of 2,200 pending causes at various stages
from introduction to canonisation.

The enduring need for miracles

The Catholic Church stands as a sign of contradiction to the modern world which has to a large extent lost its sense of mystery and miracles. The Church holds that miracles do happen. A miracle can be understood as a divine intervention which suspends the natural law. The Old Testament describes many miracles: from the creation of the universe to the parting of the Red Sea; allowing Abraham and Sarah to have a child after their child bearing years (*Gn* 17:7). This is again similar to the New Testament miracle in which Elizabeth and Zacharia produce a son, John the Baptist, after long years of not being able to conceive (*Lk* 1:7). Old Testament miracles include:

- The crossing of the Red Sea (*Ex* 14:2).
- Feeding the exiled Jewish nation under Moses with Manna and Quails (*Ex* 16:4-31, 16:13).
- Producing water from the rock at Horeb (*Ex* 17:5-7).
- Increasing the widow's oil supply (*2 K* 4:1-7).
- Curing of Naaman (*2 K* 5:1-19).

Miracles in the New Testament are seen as 'signs'. Jesus performs some 47 miracles, including exorcism, raising the dead, healing and multiplication of food. The following examples illustrate the wealth of these:

- Changing water into wine at the Wedding at Cana (*Jn* 2:1-11).
- Healing the Centurion's servant (see *Mt* 8:5-13).
- Raising Jairus' daughter to life (see *Mt* 8:28).
- Feeding the 5,000 (see *Mt* 14:1-21).

Jesus openly performed miracles during the course of His earthly ministry. These miracles or signs were designed to prove that Jesus is the son of God and thereby authenticating His mission of redemption (see: *Jn* 6:18-36, 10:24-37). The Apostolic Church was also proud to boast the signs worked by Jesus as proof of His mission and in turn of its own (see *Ac* 2:22, 10:37). Jesus gave the commission to preach His word to the disciples and apostles who went out in pairs and worked miracles in His name (see *Mk* 3:15, 16:17).

After Pentecost the Apostles went out into Jerusalem, curing the sick, casting out demons and raising the dead, all in the name of Jesus (see *Ac* 2:43, 8:7-8, 20:10).

The apostles speak widely about the miracles and signs of Jesus. On the road to Emmaus they said that Jesus was a prophet who was mighty before the people and God in words and deeds (*Lk* 24:19). St Peter describes Jesus to Cornelius as the wonder-working preacher (*Ac* 10:39).

St Paul through his missionary endeavours also cites the name of Jesus to authenticate his mission, his miracles and his discipleship (see: *Rm* 15:18-19, *Ga* 3:5, 2 *Co* 12:12).

The miracles of Jesus extend beyond the chosen people of Israel to encompass all of humanity. Jesus healed the centurion's servant and the Syro-Phoenician women (see *Mk* 7). Miracles in both the Old and New Testaments show God's power over creation, such as the Great Flood (*Gn* 7:8) and the Burning Bush (*Ex* 3:2), the plagues against Pharaoh to free an enslaved people (*Ex* 7:14-25, 11:30); Jesus also calmed the storm (*Mk* 4:35-40). There are also miracles of merciful intervention of healing, such as the curing of Naamen and of the woman with the 12 year haemorrhage (see *Mt* 9:20-22, *Mk* 5:24-34, *Lk* 8:43-48).

The miracles worked by St Paul and St Peter and the other apostles show that miracles did not stop with the ministry of Jesus and they continue today through the Church.

Requirement of miracles

The age of miracles has not passed. The requirement of a miracle confirms God's approval of the person. The Church has taken a strong line in both promoting miracles and also proving miracles. In 1088 Pope Urban II decreed that saints could not be added to the canon unless there were witnesses who declared that they had seen the miracles with their own eyes and that the Synod approved the accounts.

The Congregation of Rites in 1588 developed the requirement that miracles be subjected to a medical/legal examination. Pope Benedict XIV created a register of medical experts to examine miracles to ensure that they were inexplicable. Pope Pius XII established the Medical Commission which became the Medical Council in 1948. This Council resolved the awkward situation where theologians had to judge both the theological and medical aspect of a miracle. This reform meant that a miracle was subjected to two considerations: by medical experts and theologians - a system in place today. As the Medical Commission is concerned with science, its membership is drawn from experts in the field regardless of their faith. Their key concerns are:

i) What was the diagnosis and was it accurate and what was the prognosis and treatment provided?

ii) Was the healing rapid, complete, lasting and inexplicable according to current medical science?

The congregation then votes on the miracle and the result is passed to the Pope for determination.

Who are saints and why do we pray to them

In the Apostles' Creed we pray "I believe in the Holy Spirit, the Holy Catholic Church, and the Communion of Saints." The Creed was an early exposition of the Christian faith, before the schisms which followed, and as such it is a formula of faith accepted by most Christian churches and communities. The Creed highlights several important aspects of the Church. These are that the Church is Holy, the Church is Catholic and the Church is a Communion of saints. But what do these words Communion of Saints mean to us in the context of looking at the Catholic Church's process of beatification and canonisation?

Communion of saints

The *Catechism of the Catholic Church* describes the communion of saints as a twofold communion. It is a communion in 'Holy Things' (*Sancta*) and a communion amongst 'Holy Persons' (*Sancti*) (*CCC* 948).

Through our Baptism we become part of the Communion of Saints. The Church's traditional formula of the Church as being the Church Triumphant (in

Heaven), the Church Militant (on Earth) and the Church Suffering (in Purgatory) shows that all the baptised form part of one Church.

The Bible supports the Church's teaching on the Communion of Saints, a Communion which can be likened to a family where each member is aware of and concerned for the wellbeing of each other. This family bond is not broken by death (see *Ep* 3:14-15, *Co* 1:18-24 and *Rm* 8:35-39).

The Saints in Heaven continue their prayers for us on earth and in purgatory so that we too may enter Heaven. St Dominic the founder of the Order of Preachers (or Dominicans) said when he was dying, "Do not weep, for I shall be more useful to you after my death and I shall help you more effectively then during my life." (*CCC* 956).

Holiness

Sainthood or holiness is a concept in the Judeo-Christian tradition. In the Old Testament holiness was often seen as being set apart from others "I have made you a royal priesthood a people set apart" (*Dt* 10:8-9). Holiness in Hebrew *Quadosh* or *Qudesh* and in Greek *Hagios* is an innate characteristic of God. God is regarded as the Holy One or the One that is Holy (*Is* 1:4). And His people are called to share in this holiness (*Ex* 19:6). In the Old Testament we also see an early attempt to list the "saints" of the people. These holy people included Enoch, Noah, Moses, Aaron, Elijah, Isaiah, Hezekiah and Joshua (*Qo* 44-49).

Through baptism we become children of God and inherit eternal life with Him in Heaven. The word Holy and the word Saint are essentially one and the same: the person or thing is holy and dedicated to God. Often the words are translated as being Saint in the New Testament and Holy One in the Old Testament. We see in scripture the vitality of the understanding of sainthood and holiness. The Psalms say "I will sing praises to thee with the lyre, O Holy One of Israel." (*Ps* 71:22). The New Testament uses the term Holy One to describe Jesus: "You have the words of eternal life; and we have believed, and have come to know, that you are the Holy One of God." (*Jn* 6:67-69). The New Testament describes the living and dead who have followed Christ as saints. St Paul writes of himself: "Paul an apostle of Christ Jesus by the will of God, and Timothy our brother. To all the church of God which is at Corinth, with all the saints who are in the whole of Achaia." (2 *Co* 1:1) Here St Paul greets all the assembly of Christ as being saints, 'Holy Persons' set aside as being holy through their baptism. In his letter to the Philippians he addresses the assembly of the Church in a similar manner (1:1).

In the Gospel of Matthew after the crucifixion we see that the saints in their tombs are raised and go into Jerusalem (*Mt* 27:52-53).

Veneration of the saints is evidenced in the scriptures, and from the early days of the Christian community. We see that the life and death of the martyrs were recorded by the Church: as early as 115AD we have the commemoration of the martyrdom of St Polycarp.

Why should we pray through or for others?

The word pray means to ask for something; it is a request or petition for a favour or a grant of request. For instance, in court papers we often read the phrase 'my client prays that the court will do x, y or z.' This is not deification of the court, it merely means the client asks the court to grant an order in their favour. Prayer only became restricted to worship at the time of the reformation. So understood in the fuller Catholic understanding of the word, to pray to a saint is not to accord worship to the saint. We are merely asking them for help. The story of Dives and Lazarus shows that the dead are aware of what happens on earth after their death. Dives attempts to intercede on behalf of his relatives on earth (from his place in Hell) - so even those in Hell are aware of things on earth (*Lk* 16:19-31).

Scripture rightly accords sole mediatorship to Jesus. St Paul writes "For there is one God, and there is one mediator between God and Men, the Man Christ Jesus." (1 *Tm* 2:5). This is not contradicted by the encouragement to pray for the intercession of the Saints. Jesus is the judge of our life and he determines what will become of us after death. The intercession on our behalf by an advocate does not diminish the role of the judge in deciding the outcome of a case. St Paul clearly promotes the correctness of praying for others and calls for prayers for himself and his ministry. Praying for each other is part of the Christian life (1 *Tm* 2:1-4). Paul asks the saints to pray for him in several of his letters (see *Rm* 15:30-32, *Ep* 6:18-20, *Col* 4:3, 1 *Th* 5:25, 2 *Th* 3:1).

Jesus

Critically, Jesus Himself required His followers to pray for others (*Mt* 5:44). Throughout the Gospels Jesus demonstrated a willingness to act in favour of someone on the intercession of a third person (*Mt* 8:13). Thus, those more advanced in the faith can support those in need. The New Testament teaches that those in heaven are more perfected in holiness then those on earth (*Heb* 12:22-23). The Old Testament likewise shows the efficacy of prayer. Elijah is reported as having prayed that it would not rain for three years and it did not; he

then prayed for rain and the rains came (*Jm* 5:16-18).
Abraham, the great common patriarch of the Judeo-
Christian tradition, asked an angel to intercede for him
and his prayers were answered (*Gn* 48:16). The Old
Testament shows other examples of intercessory prayer
being accepted by God. Abraham prays for the healing of
Abimlech and his household, and is answered (*Gn*
20:17). God also answered the intercessory payers of
Moses (see *Ex* 32:11-14, Nb 14:17-20).

St Paul

Intercessory prayer is urged by St Paul who writes: "I
urge that supplications, prayers, intercessions, and
thanksgivings be made for all men... This is good and
pleasing to God our saviour, who desires all men to be
saved and to come to knowledge of the truth (1 *Tm* 2:1-
4)". Thus asking for intercessory prayers from those in
heaven is not prohibited by the Old Testament rule
against necromancy - conjuring up the dead (*Dt* 18:10-
11). As with intercessory prayers, we are asking the
saints to bring our concerns before the throne of God.
And indeed the saints are not dead, as they live in
paradise with God. We know that they live: Jesus held a
conversation, in the presence of his apostles with Moses
and Elijah (*Mt* 17:3).

We know from the Book of Revelation that the prayers of the saints come before the God (*Rv* 8:3-4). It is also clear that these prayers are not just the prayers of angels as St John records that he saw "...twenty-four elders fall down before the Lamb, each holding a harp. And with golden bowls full of incense, which are the prayers of the saints (*Rv* 5:8)". As the Gospel of John shows, these prayers to intercessors do not diminish the need to have confidence in prayers directly to Jesus (*Jn* 14:13-14).

The Mass

We see that the intercessory prayer to the saints is a key part of the Roman Canon of the Mass, during which the priests prays:

> "In union with the whole Church we honour Mary, the ever-virgin mother of Jesus Christ our Lord and God. We honour Joseph, her husband, the apostles and martyrs Peter and Paul, Andrew, [James, John, Thomas, James, Philip, Bartholomew, Matthew, Simon and Jude; we honour Linus, Cletus, Clement, Sixtus, Cornelius, Cyprian, Lawrence, Chrysogonus, John and Paul, Cosmas and Damian] and all the saints. May their merits and prayers gain us your constant help and protection. Through Christ our Lord. Amen."

Through this prayer the priest joins the prayers of those at the Mass to the prayers of these holy men and women, apostles and early martyrs. The priest continues:

"Look with favour on these offerings and accept them as once you accepted the gifts of your servant Abel, the sacrifice of Abraham, our father in faith and the bread and wine offered by your priest Melchizedek. Almighty God, we pray that your angel may take this sacrifice to your altar in Heaven."

These prayers, the Book of Revelation insists will come before God. The process of beatification and canonisation is a mechanism to enable the Church to hold out with confidence examples of the Christian life for us to imitate and have confidence in. Therefore we may seek the intercessory prayers which Jesus encourages us to make with confidence. It is God who has formed the person into a saint. The Church provides, through its sacraments, the tools to do so.

Bibliography

Motu proprio *Sancitita clarior*, 1969.

Motu proprio *Mysterii Paschalis* 1969.

The Apostolic Constitution *Divinus Perfectionis Magister*, 1983.

New Laws for the Causes of Saints, Sacred Congregation for the Causes of Saints, 1983.

Communiqué of the Congregation for the Causes of Saints on *New Procedures in the Rite of Beatification*, 2005.

Instruction *Sanctorum Mater*, On the Procedures of Diocesan and Eparchial Enquiries for the Causes of Saints, Congregation for the Causes of Saints, 2008.

Matthew Bunson, *John Paul II's Book of Saints* (Hardcover), Our Sunday Visitor, 2007.

Ann Ball, *Modern Saints: Their Lives and Faces,* Book One (Paperback), Tan Books, 1991.

Modern Saints: Their Lives and Faces, Book Two (Paperback), Atlantic Books, 1991.

Joan Carrol Cruz, *Secular Saints: 250 Canonised and Beatified Lay Men Women and Children*, Tan Books, 1989.

The Incorruptibles: A Study of the Incorruption of the Bodies of Various Saints and Beati, Tan Books, 1982.

Saintly Women of Modern Times, Our Sunday Visitor, 2004.

Saintly Men of Modern Times, Our Sunday Visitor, 2003.

Saintly Youth of Modern Times, Our Sunday Visitor, 2006.

Relics, Our Sunday Visitor, 1984.

Ferdinand Holbeck, *New Saints and Blesseds of the Catholic Church 1979-1983*, Ignatius Press, 2000.

New Saints and Blesseds of the Catholic Church 1983-1987, Ignatius Press, 2003.

Married Saints and Blesseds through the Centuries, Ignatius Press, 2002.

Robert Royal, *Catholic Martyrs of the 20th Century: A Comprehensive World History*, Crossroad General Interests, 2000.

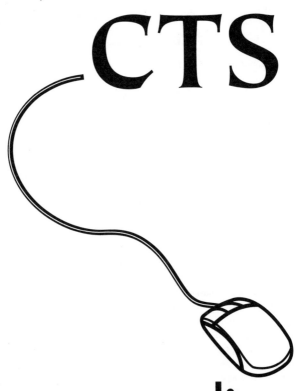

CTS

... now online
www.cts-online.org.uk